T4-ADX-682

WHAT REALLY HAPPENED?

The True Story of the EMANCIPATION PROCLAMATION

Willow Clark

Fitchburg Public Library
5530 Lacy Road
Fitchburg, WI 53711

PowerKiDS press

New York

WITHDRAWN

Published in 2013 by The Rosen Publishing Group, Inc.
29 East 21st Street, New York, NY 10010

Copyright © 2013 by The Rosen Publishing Group, Inc.

All rights reserved. No part of this book may be reproduced in any form without permission in writing from the publisher, except by a reviewer.

First Edition

Editor: Amelie von Zumbusch
Book Design: Colleen Bialecki

Photo Credits: Cover © Everett Col. Collection/age fotostock; p. 5 Hulton Archive/Getty Images; p. 7 Photo Researchers/Getty Images; pp. 9, 15 FPG/Taxi/Getty Images; pp. 11, 17, 19 MPI/Stringer/Archive Photos/Getty Images; p. 13 *The Hour of Emancipation*, 1863, Carlton, William Tolman (1816–1888)/Private Collections/Photo © Christine's Images/The Bridgeman Art Library; p. 21 *On to Liberty*, 1867, Kaufman, Theodore (1814–1887)/Private Collection/Photo © Christine's Images/The Bridgeman Art Library.

Library of Congress Cataloging-in-Publication Data

Clark, Willow.
 The true story of the Emancipation Proclamation / by Willow Clark. — 1st ed.
   p. cm. — (What really happened?)
 Includes index.
 ISBN 978-1-4488-9695-0 (library binding) — ISBN 978-1-4488-9848-0 (pbk.) —
 ISBN 978-1-4488-9849-7 (6-pack)
 1. United States. President (1861–1865 : Lincoln). Emancipation Proclamation—Juvenile literature. 2. Slaves—Emancipation—United States—Juvenile literature. 3. United States—History—Civil War, 1861–1865—Sources—Juvenile literature. 4. United States—Politics and government—1861–1865—Juvenile literature. I. Title.
 E453.C534 2013
 973.7'14—dc23

2012034154

Manufactured in the United States of America

CPSIA Compliance Information: Batch #W13PK4: For Further Information contact Rosen Publishing, New York, New York at 1-800-237-9932

CONTENTS

Emancipation at Last 4
Slavery 6
War Breaks Out 8
Two Years of War 10
What Does It Say? 12
A Change of Focus 14
The Worldwide Impact 16
Fighting for Freedom 18
After the War 20
What Really Happened? 22
Glossary 23
Index 24
Websites 24

EMANCIPATION AT LAST

In the mid-nineteenth century, most African Americans were slaves. On January 1, 1863, President Abraham Lincoln issued the Emancipation Proclamation. This **executive order** freed slaves that were living in the Confederate states. These were states that **seceded**, or broke away from the Union, in 1861. This led to the Civil War. The Emancipation Proclamation also said that African Americans could join the Union army and help fight the war.

The Emancipation Proclamation was important. It changed the focus of the Civil War from keeping the United States together to bringing an end to slavery. However, people often misunderstand this **document** today.

A proclamation is an official public announcement of something. The word "emancipation" means "setting free." It is most often used to refer to slaves being freed.

SLAVERY

African slaves were first brought to the English colonies that would become the United States in 1619. Slavery was legal throughout Colonial times and after the American Revolution.

By the nineteenth century, the **economies** of southern states relied on slaves. The economies of northern states did not. Northern states began to **abolish**, or outlaw, slavery. States where slavery was legal became known as slave states, while states where slavery was illegal were called free states.

Life as a slave was hard. Slaves were whipped and mistreated in other ways. Slave owners could sell their slaves at any time, breaking up slave families.

Dred Scott tried to win his freedom in court. The case reached the Supreme Court in 1857. It decided that slaves and their descendants were not citizens. Scott remained a slave.

WAR BREAKS OUT

In the nineteenth century, the United States grew quickly. Politicians fought over whether new states would be free states or slave states. Both sides made **compromises**, but the relationship between the North and South kept getting tenser.

In 1860, four men ran in the presidential election. The winner was Abraham Lincoln, who opposed the spread of slavery. Soon after Lincoln's election, South Carolina seceded from the Union. Mississippi, Florida, Alabama, Georgia, Louisiana, and Texas soon followed. These states formed the Confederate States of America. The Civil War started when Confederate forces attacked the Union-held Fort Sumter, in Charleston, South Carolina, on April 12, 1861.

Lincoln thought slavery was wrong and was against letting it spread. However, he originally said that keeping the country together, rather than ending slavery, should be the goal of the Civil War.

TWO YEARS OF WAR

After the Battle of Fort Sumter, Virginia, North Carolina, Arkansas, and Tennessee seceded and joined the Confederacy. At first, both sides thought that the war would end quickly. However, it was still going on in September 1862, when the Battle of Antietam was fought. It was the bloodiest single-day battle of the war, leaving around 23,000 **casualties**. Neither side really won, but the Union claimed a victory because they stopped the Confederates' push north.

After Antietam, Lincoln issued a **preliminary** version of the Emancipation Proclamation. This said that slaves in states that were still rebelling against the Union would be declared free on January 1, 1863.

The Battle of Antietam is also known as the Battle of Sharpsburg. It was fought in Sharpsburg, Maryland, along Antietam Creek.

WHAT DOES IT SAY?

Abraham Lincoln issued the Emancipation Proclamation on January 1, 1863. It stated that "all persons held as slaves" within any state or part of a state that was "in rebellion against the United States, shall be then, thenceforward, and forever free." It also said that African Americans could join the Union army.

The Emancipation Proclamation did not end slavery everywhere. It did not free slaves in border states, or slave states that did not secede from the Union. It also did not free slaves in Confederate areas that were under Union control. However, it tied the issue of ending slavery to the Union winning the war.

These slaves are learning about the Emancipation Proclamation. Slaves welcomed the news, even though it left about 1 million people within the Union as slaves.

A CHANGE OF FOCUS

Although the Emancipation Proclamation did not end slavery, it changed the focus of the Civil War for the Union. The North had entered into the war to keep Southern states from seceding. Now the North was fighting both to preserve the Union and to end slavery.

While some Union soldiers disliked the idea of abolishing slavery, many were inspired by the sense that they were now fighting for a good cause. Abolitionists, or people who wanted to abolish slavery throughout the country, celebrated the Emancipation Proclamation. They understood that it was a step toward ending slavery, even if it did not do so everywhere.

Abolitionists, such as Frederick Douglass, had wanted abolition to be the goal of the war all along. Douglass was an abolitionist leader who had been born a slave.

THE WORLDWIDE IMPACT

    The Emancipation Proclamation affected the Union's relationships with foreign countries, such as Great Britain. The Union and the Confederacy both wanted supplies from other countries. In fact, British merchants supplied the Confederacy with guns and warships. However, the Confederacy wanted Great Britain and other countries to **recognize** it officially as an independent country.

    When the Emancipation Proclamation shifted the focus of the war to slavery, Great Britain decided it would not recognize the Confederacy because that would make it look like it supported slavery. In this way, the Emancipation Proclamation struck an important blow to the Confederate cause.

In 1864, a Union ship, the Kearsarge, sunk a Confederate ship, the Alabama, off the coast of France. Before the battle, the Kearsarge sailed out of French waters to avoid bringing France into the war.

FIGHTING FOR FREEDOM

Once the Emancipation Proclamation allowed African Americans to fight for the Union, many were eager to enlist. They were formed into all-black units. By the time the war ended, in 1865, nearly 200,000 African Americans had joined the Army.

The most famous group of African American soldiers was the 54th Massachusetts Volunteer Infantry. They became known for their heroism as well as for standing up to the unfair treatment they faced. African American soldiers were paid less than white soldiers. To protest against this, the entire 54th regiment refused to accept their wages until the Army agreed to pay black and white soldiers equally.

The 54th Massachusetts Volunteer Infantry fought in several battles, including the Second Battle of Fort Wagner, seen here. The 1989 movie *Glory* was based on the experiences of men in this regiment.

AFTER THE WAR

The Civil War ended when the Confederacy surrendered to the Union on April 9, 1865. In the years that followed, there were several **amendments**, or changes, to the **Constitution**. The Thirteenth Amendment finally outlawed slavery throughout the country. Former slaves were made citizens by the Fourteenth Amendment. The Fifteenth Amendment granted voting rights to former slaves who were adult males.

Although these amendments were now part of the Constitution, state and local laws allowed unfair treatment of African Americans to continue. These were known as Jim Crow laws. Many of them were not struck down until the civil rights movement in the 1960s.

During the war, many slaves escaped to Union army camps. This became more common later in the war, as the Union army advanced deep into the South.

WHAT REALLY HAPPENED?

What we know about the Emancipation Proclamation and its effects comes from many sources. First, we have Lincoln's words themselves. Then, we have everything that Lincoln, his advisors, and people involved on both sides of the war wrote in reaction to this document. Drawing on all these different sources helps us understand the reasons Lincoln issued the proclamation and the many effects it had.

Even so, people often misunderstand the Emancipation Proclamation as freeing all the slaves. A careful reading shows that is not the case. Looking more closely at the original sources gives us a better understanding of what really happened.

GLOSSARY

abolish (uh-BAH-lish) To do away with.

amendments (uh-MEND-ments) Additions or changes to the Constitution.

casualties (KA-zhul-teez) People who are injured or killed in an accident or a war.

compromises (KOM-pruh-myz-ez) Agreements reached by both sides giving up something.

Constitution (kon-stih-TOO-shun) The basic rules by which the United States is governed.

document (DOK-yoo-ment) A written or printed statement that gives official information about something.

economies (ih-KAH-nuh-meez) The ways in which countries or businesses oversee their goods and services.

executive order (eg-ZEK-yoo-tiv OR-der) An official command from the president.

preliminary (prih-LIH-muh-ner-ee) Leading up to something.

recognize (REH-kig-nyz) To accept officially.

seceded (sih-SEED-ed) Withdrew from a group or a country.

INDEX

A
army, 4, 12, 18

C
Civil War, 4, 8, 14, 20
Constitution, 20

D
document, 4, 22

E
economies, 6

end, 4
executive order, 4

F
families, 6
focus, 4, 14, 16

L
Lincoln, Abraham, 4, 8, 10, 12, 22

N
North, 8, 14

P
politicians, 8

S
side(s), 8, 10, 22
slave owners, 6
South, 8

U
Union, 4, 8, 10, 12, 14, 16, 18, 20
United States, 4, 6, 8, 12

WEBSITES

Due to the changing nature of Internet links, PowerKids Press has developed an online list of websites related to the subject of this book. This site is updated regularly. Please use this link to access the list:
www.powerkidslinks.com/wrh/empro/

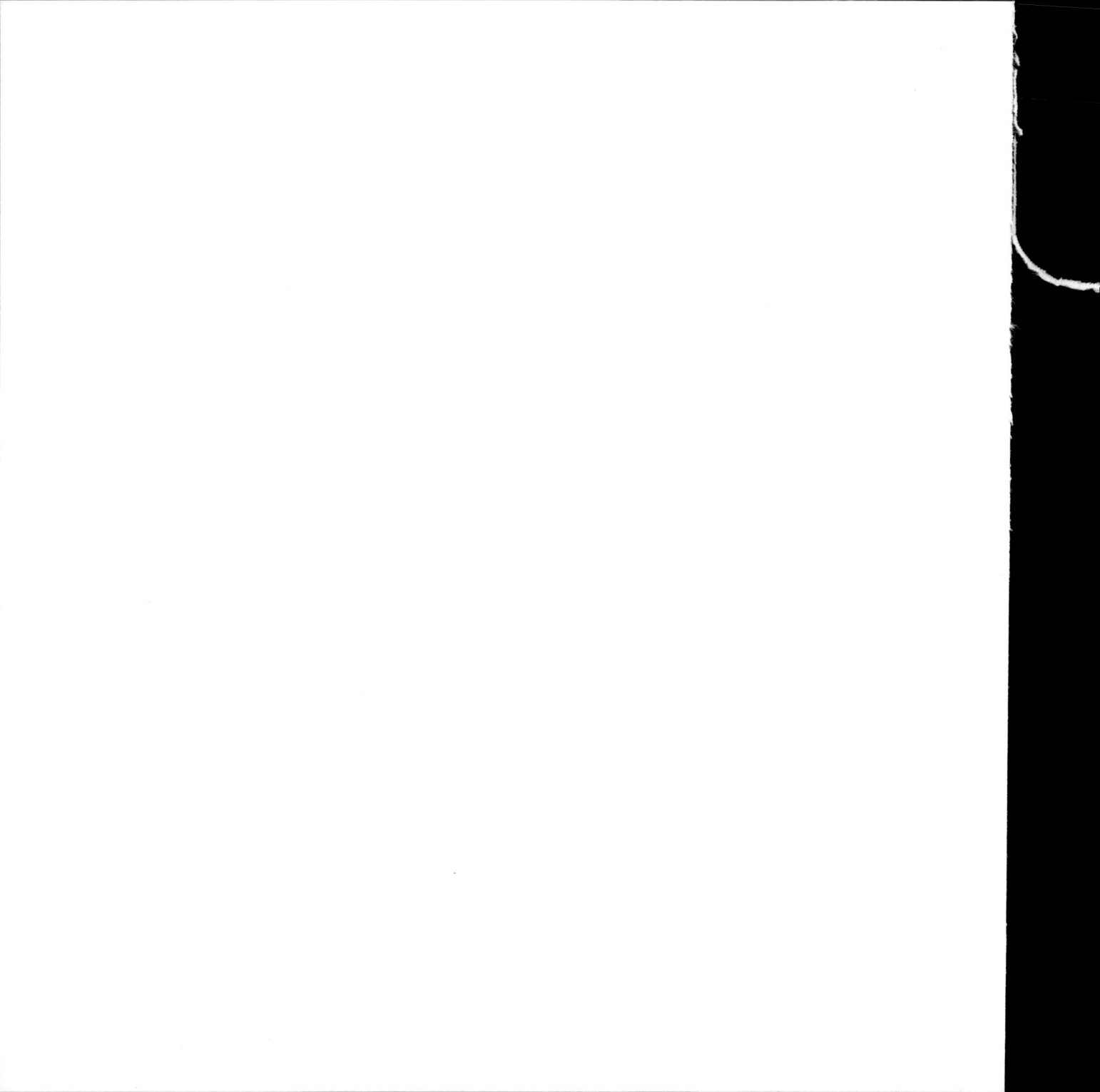